The New Reading Hebrew

A Guided Instruction Course

Dr. C. Castberg and Lillian W. Adler

Design: Pronto Design Inc.
Original Concept: Stephen Kraft

Copyright © 2004 Behrman House, Inc.
Millburn, NJ 07081
ISBN 13: 978-0-87441-728-9

Behrman House, Inc.
www.behrmanhouse.com

New Letters and Vowels   Lesson

		בּ ב	1
ד	ךּ		2
	שֹׁ	שׁ	3
	תּ	ת	4
	ל	מ	5
וֹ	וֹ	ם	6
ן	י	ו	7
	ע	א	8
	ג	נ	9
ה	ח		10
ך	בּ	כ	11
	יָ		12
	פֿ	פ	13
	ט	ק	14
ז	ץ	צ	15
ף		ס	16

Turn the page to begin
Lessons 1, 2, 3, and 4.

Begin Lesson 1 Here

You are about to learn the Hebrew alphabet in a very easy way. Let us show you just how easy it is. Look at these two letters:

B ‎ב

One of these is English. The other is the *Hebrew* form of the *same* letter. Copy the English one here: _____

TURN THE PAGE TO CHECK YOUR ANSWER.

Begin Lesson 2 Here

In Lesson 1, you learned two letters and one vowel. Let's review them.

This Hebrew letter ‎ב is called **BET** and has the saying sound of _____ .

TURN THE PAGE TO CHECK YOUR ANSWER.

Begin Lesson 3 Here

In this lesson, you will learn two new letters that look like flowers in pots.

Here they are: ‎שׂ ‎שׁ

SIN   SHIN

The letter with the dot on the right is called _____ .

TURN THE PAGE TO CHECK YOUR ANSWER.

Begin Lesson 4 Here

You have learned that two different vowels, ַ and ָ, have the same sound: AH as in OOMPAH.

Now you will learn that two *letters* can have the same sound, and have the same name as well. ‎ת and ‎תּ are both **TAHV**.

Though one has a dot and the other doesn't, the name of both ‎ת and ‎תּ is _____ .

TURN THE PAGE TO CHECK YOUR ANSWER.

PURIM

פּוּרִים

Another lesson finished!

In Lesson 13, you learned that PAY פ has the saying sound of P, that FAY פ has the saying sound of F, and that ֻ is the vowel U as in PUT.

TURN BACK TO PAGE 97 TO BEGIN LESSON 14.

יוֹם טוֹב

YOM TOV

טוֹב, טוֹב!

You've learned that KOOF ק , written below the line, has the saying sound of K

and that TET ט has the saying sound of T.

TURN BACK TO PAGE 97 TO BEGIN LESSON 15.

8

One more lesson to go!

In Lesson 15, you learned that

צ is TSAHDEE,

ץ is FINAL TSAHDEE, and

ז is ZAHYIN.

TURN BACK TO PAGE 97 TO BEGIN LESSON 16.

SOF

סוֹף

("END"!)

Congratulations!

מַזָל טוֹב!

Check your answer here:

B

Have you checked your answer? Good. Always do this—even when you know you are right. It will help you to remember the correct answer. Oh, by the way, you've learned your first Hebrew letter, ב. It has the same sound as the English letter _____ .

(WRITE YOUR ANSWER. THEN TURN THE PAGE AGAIN.)

Check your answer here:

B

When you see ב, you know it has the saying sound of _____ and is called _____ .

Check your answer here:

SHIN ש

Our two new letters are **SIN** and **SHIN**.

This letter ש is called _____ .

Check your answer here:

TAHV

ת and תּ

תּ and ת have the same name.

Both are **TAHV**.

Though תּ has a dot and ת has no dot, we call them by the same name: _____ .

פּוּרִים

POO-REEM

(Commonly spelled PURIM)

This holiday פּוּרִים is _____ .

חַג   CHAHG

You might have used ָ ,
but in this word we use ַ .

Here is another way to say HOLIDAY:

יוֹם טוֹב

Write the sounds here: _____ _____

V

Put a circle around each ZAHYIN:

ז ז ז ז ז ז ז ז ז ז ז ז ז ז ז ז

How many circles did you draw? _____

SO   סוֹ

When you read this word, you will have completed
READING HEBREW, and have come to the END.

סוֹף

_____

B

This is how to write a Hebrew **B**:

ב step 3   ב step 2   ך step 1   ← **start here**

Now you try it:

_____ 3   _____ 2   _____ 1

B
BET   בּ

This is **BET** בּ. **VET** is written like this: ב, and has no dot in the middle. Because the name of a letter begins with its saying sound, you know that **VET** has the saying sound of _____ .

SHIN   שׁ

We know that this letter שׁ is **SHIN**, and this letter שׂ is _____ .

TAHV

ת and תּ

VET ב has no dot and has the sound **V**.

BET בּ has a dot and has the sound **B**.

The dot gives the letter a new name and sound.

The dot *doesn't* change the sound of **TAHV**, though.

ת and תּ have the _____ sound.

POO   פ

Let's combine POO פ with REEM רים, to form

פוּרִים,

and we have the name of a holiday: _____ .

ג ח ב ס י

G CH V M Y

In Hebrew, there are several words for **HOLIDAY**.

One word is **CHAHG**. Fill in the correct vowel to make this word **CHAHG**:

חג

ZAHYIN   ז

ז has the saying sound of **Z**.

ז has the saying sound of _____ .

S

Combine **SAHMECH** ס with the vowel וֹ (**O** as in **TORAH**), like this: סוֹ, and we read _____ .

בּ בּ ר

Good! You've learned to write the Hebrew way—from RIGHT to LEFT. Write a בּ in the right-hand circle:

◯　　◯

ָ

You have learned a vowel with the sound **AY** as in **DAY**.

Write it here, below the line: _____

SIN　שׂ

We recognize the letter **SHIN** שׁ because it has a dot on the _____ side.

same

Say the names of these letters aloud:

תּ ב בּ ת ⟵

Now go back and circle the two letters called **TAHV**.

REEM ריִם

When we combine פ and the vowel O וֹ, like this: פוֹ, the sound is PO.

This sound פוֹ is _____ .

TOV טוֹב

Let's review some letters we learned before.

Under each letter, write its saying sound:

GIMMEL	CHET	VET	FINAL MEM	YUD
ג	ח	ב	ם	י
___	___	___	___	___

#2 and #6 ז וֹ

Sometimes ז and ו are mistaken for one another.

You know that this ו is VAHV.

This ז is _____ , and it always has a slanted head.

#3 ך

FINAL MEM ם looks very much like SAHMECH ס.

ס has the saying sound of ____ .

One of these arrows shows the correct way to read and write Hebrew.

Label it "בִ":

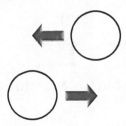

AY

The vowel ‥ has the sound AY as in DAY.

When we combine בּ and ‥ as בֵּ, we get the sound BAY.

So, בֵ has the sound _____.

right

The name of this Hebrew letter שׁ is _____.

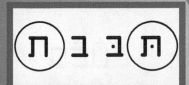

This letter with the dot תּ is _____.

Without the dot ת, it is still called _____.

חָכָם

You remember that רֵי is read REE.

Add the **FINAL MEM** ם to רֵי, like this: רֵים.

The sound is _____ .

בוּ
(2)

VOO

Ready to read the Hebrew word "good"?

טוֹב

The sound is _____ .

ZAHYIN

Z

ז

Which two sounds below read **ZAH**?

זָ (6)　　זֵ (5)　　זוֹ (4)　　זֵ (3)　　זָ (2)　　זוֹ (1)

#____ and #____

FINAL

MEM

ם

Which **FINAL LETTER** has the saying sound of **F**?

ץ (4)　　ף (3)　　ד (2)　　ן (1)

#____

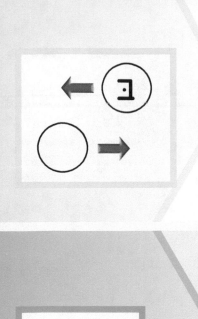

This letter בּ is the Hebrew _____ .

VAY

בֵּ

To sum up all we've learned:

The sound of this letter and vowel בֵּ is _____ .

The sound of this letter and vowel בֵ is _____ .

SHIN

שׁ

The name of the letter שׁ is SHIN.

Since the saying sound of a Hebrew letter is always the first sound of its name, the saying sound of שׁ is _____ .

TAHV

TAHV

תּ

ת

We know that the name of a Hebrew letter always starts with its saying sound. The saying sound of the letter TAHV ת is _____ .

חָ and כָ both have the sound CHAH.

Fill in the 2 vowels that will make this word read CHACHAM, meaning "wise."

CHACHAM ⁢חכם

חָ כָ

CHAH CHAH
(2) (1)

TOO BIH-SHVAHT
(commonly spelled
TU B'SHVAT)

One of these syllables reads VOO. Which one?

טוֹ בּוּ מוֹ
(3) (2) (1)

Your answer: _____

ZAHYIN ז

ז is called _____ and has the saying sound of _____.

FINAL FAY
F
ף

You remember that four (4) FINAL letters are written partly below the line:

CHAHF ך, NUN ן, TSAHDEE ץ, and FAY ף.

One FINAL LETTER ם is written *on* the line.

ם is the FINAL _____.

B

The Hebrew letter בּ will have the sound of **B**.

We will refer to the sound of a letter as the "saying sound."

So—the "saying sound" of this letter is _____ .

BAY

VAY

בֵּ

Let's practice reading sounds you know aloud:

בֵּ   בֵ   בֵּ   בֵּ   בֵּ   ⟵ **start here**

How many times did you read **VAY**? _____

SH

Let's practice writing the **SHIN**:

שׁ step 3   ש step 2   ⌐ step 1

We'll do one, then you do the next three:

שׁ

_____   _____   _____   שׁ

T

תּ also has the saying sound of **T** and is called _____ .

Both of these syllables read **CHAH**.

Under each one, write its correct sound:

נַ   חַ

_____   _____

(2)   (1)

נַ   **NU**

TEH   שְׁ

This letter and vowel combination טוּ reads _____,
as in the holiday _____ **BIH-SHVAHT**.

Z

This letter ז, with the saying sound of **Z**, is called _____.

(Notice the slanted head!)

F

This letter ף is called _____ _____ and has
the saying sound of _____.

B

When you see this letter ⅃, you will know that its
"_____ing sound" is B.

3

If you've scored 100% on Lesson 2 so far, you're ready to go
on. If not, go back to Lesson 2: Frame 1 and review each
frame until your score is perfect.

If you are ready to learn two new vowels, answer yes: _____

ש ש ש

Whenever you see either of these letters, ש or ש, you
know that SIN has the dot on the left side.

Copy the letter SIN: _____

TAHV ת

ת and תֿ both have the saying sound of T.

The name of both ת and תֿ is _____, and both have
the saying sound of _____.

Our vowels:

AH　AH　EH　IH　ᵉEE　U　AY　O◌ֹ　OO◌וּ
◌ָ　◌ַ　◌ֶ　◌ִ　◌ִ　◌ֻ　◌ֵ

Read the letters and vowels below, then copy the one with the sound **NU**:

וֹי　פוֹ　כָ　נֻ　חַ

_____

✓ ✓
תֻ　תֻ　**TU**

ⓜ **MEM**

ט **TET**

This letter and vowel combination מֶ reads **MEH**.

This syllable טֶ reads _____ .

ZAHYIN

ז

The letter **ZAHYIN** ז has the saying sound of _____ .

---

below

The saying sound of **FINAL FAY** ף is _____ .

"saying sound"

Hebrew letters have names.

The name of this letter בּ is BET.

Write the letter BET here: _____

YES

(That was easy, wasn't it?)

Here are the two new vowels: _____ _____

Both are written below the line and have the same sound: AH as in OOMPAH.

The two vowels _____ and _____ have the same sound, AH as in OOMPAH, and are written _____ the line.

שׂ SIN

Did you remember to put the dot on the left?

In the circle, write the SHIN: ◯

In the square, write the SIN: ☐

TAHV

T

תּ ת

Let's practice writing the TAHV תּ:

תּ step 3   ת step 2   ⊤ step 1

_____ _____ תּ

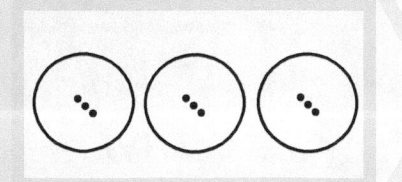

Let's combine letters we know with the new vowel U as in PUT.

Put a ✔ over the syllables that read TU:

תֻ   תֻ   בֻ   בֻ   פֻ   פֻ

5

In the circle, write **MEM**: ◯

In the square, write **TET**: ☐

ץ

FINAL TSAHDEE

We have not studied one of these letters. Which one?

ת   ש   ז   ו   ל

TAHV   SHIN   ZAHYIN   VAHV   LAHMED

_____

ף ף ף

You know that the **FINAL FAY** ף dips partly

_____ the line and appears only at the end of a word.

ב   BET

The saying sound of the letter ב, whose name is BET, is _____ .

below

There are two vowels, ַ and ָ , with the sound AH as in OOMPAH.

Circle the vowel that does *not* have the sound AH as in OOMPAH:

ַ   ֵ   ָ

שׁ   SHIN

שׂ   SIN

The name of this letter שׁ , with the saying sound of S, is _____ .

ת ת ת

When we practice this letter ת without the dot, we are still writing the letter called _____ . Write a few below:

_____   _____   _____   _ ת _

U

Circle each vowel that has the sound **U** below:

TET

ט

Put a ✔ over each **TET** below:

ט מ ט ט מ ט ט

How many did you ✔? _____

end

The name of this letter ץ is

_____ _____.

(2)

ף

FINAL FAY ף is written this way:

ף step 2   ף step 1

Now you:

____ ____ ____ ף

B

The letter BET בּ has the

s__________ s__________ of B.

ֵ AY

Our two new vowels have the same sound:

AH as in OOMPAH.

We write AH as in OOMPAH below the line, either this way ַ or this way ָ.

Copy the vowels that have the sound AH as in OOMPAH:

ַ ֵ ָ ___ ___

SIN שׂ

The saying sound of SIN is ____.

We write SIN: ____.

TAHV
ת ת ת

When we add the vowel AH ַ as in OOMPAH to ת, like this: תַ, we read TAH.

Using the same vowel ַ, write TAH another way:

____

U as in PUT ֻ

The vowel **U** as in **PUT** is written _____ .

ט ט ט

Some people confuse **TET** ט and **MEM** מ.

We know that the letter with the opening at the bottom מ is **MEM**.

This letter ט, open at the top, is _____ .

ץ ץ ץ

The **FINAL TSAHDEE** ץ dips partly below the line and appears only at the _____ of a word.

סֵפֶר

Just one more letter to learn, and you'll know the entire Hebrew alphabet!

One of the letters below is the **FINAL FAY**.

Which number is the **FINAL FAY**?

(2)   (1)

(   )   ף   פ

saying sound

The name of this letter ⅃ is _____ .

— ⊤ AH

This vowel — and this vowel ⊤, written below the line, have the same sound.

The sound of both vowels is _____ as in _____ .

S
Ⱶ

Ⱶ is called _____ and has the saying sound of _____ .

תּ TAH

This vowel ⊤ is also AH as in OOMPAH.

The sound of this letter and vowel תּ is

_____ .

PUT

∴ is a vowel that has the sound _____ as in _____ .

ּ

We'll practice writing the **TET** ט:

ט step 3   ט step 2   ד step 1

Now you:

___ ___ ___ _ט_

✓
ץ

This is the way we write the **FINAL TSAHDEE**:

ץ step 2   ן step 1

___ ___ ___ _ץ_

פֶּסַח

One of these words is the Hebrew word for "**BOOK**."

סֵדֶר   פֶּסַח   סֵפֶר

PESACH

You might have used ָ ,
but in this word we use ַ .

Copy it here: _____

BET ‏ב‏

The name of a Hebrew letter *always* starts with its saying sound. The saying sound of the letter BET is _____.

AH as in OOMPAH

You remember that ‏ַ‏ and ‏ָ‏ have the sound AH as in OOMPAH, and ‏ֵ‏ has the sound AY as in DAY.

Practice reading these vowels aloud:

‏ֵ‏   ‏ַ‏   ‏ֵ‏   ‏ֵ‏   ‏ָ‏   ‏ַ‏   ‏ֵ‏   **← start here**

How many have the sound AH? _____

SIN
S

‏שׂ‏

How many times does SHIN appear in the line below?

‏שׁ‏   ‏שׁ‏   ‏שׁ‏   ‏שׁ‏   ‏שׁ‏   ‏שׁ‏

Write your answer here: _____

TAH ‏תָּ‏

You know two ways to write the sound T.

You know two vowels that have the sound AH as in OOMPAH.

You should be able to write the sound TAH four different ways! Try it here, in any order:

_____   _____   _____   _____
4   3   2   1

_____ ‧ּ   U

The vowel ‧ּ has the sound **U** as in _____ .

TAHV   תּ

Both **TET** ט and **TAHV** תּ have the saying sound of _____ .

צַדִיק

TSAHDEEK

One of these letters is new: _ץ_   צ

The new letter is **FINAL TSAHDEE**.

Put a ✓ over the **FINAL TSAHDEE**:

_ץ_   צ

סֵדֶר

SAYDER
(commonly spelled
SEDER)

The **SEDER** סֵדֶר takes place on the holiday of
PEH-SAHCH (commonly spelled **PESACH**).

Fill in the correct vowels to make this word read **PESACH**:

פסח

B

The Hebrew letter בּ has the saying sound of B.

If we leave out the dot ב, the letter has the saying sound of V.

In the space below, copy the letter with the saying sound of V.

_____

3

When we combine the sounds B בּ and AH ַ , we make the sound BAH בַּ.

This letter and vowel make the sound

_____ .

4

Helpful hints: ֵ is the vowel AY as in DAY.

ָ and ַ are the vowels AH as in OOMPAH.

Draw a circle around the letter and vowel that reads SHAH:

         שֵׁ

Your sounds should include all of these. (If they don't, go back to Lesson 4: Frame 1 and review.)

This vowel ֵ is AY as in DAY.

Read each of these sounds aloud, then draw a circle around every TAY:

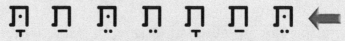 ←

How many did you circle? _____

ב CH
ת T
ב V

Another "last" to learn—this time the last vowel.

It's written under the line.

＿＿ is **U** as in **PUT**.

U as in **PUT** is written: ＿＿＿

ט TET
✓

ט is called **TET**, and ת is called ＿＿＿＿＿＿＿ .

צַדִי

TSAHDEE

We'll add the **KOOF** ק to the צַ and דִי , like this: צַדִיק , and we create the Hebrew word for "**RIGHTEOUS**."

Write its sound here: ＿＿＿＿＿＿＿＿＿

סֵפֶר

SAYFER

You know that the word for "**BOOK**" is **SAYFER** סֵפֶר .

Substitute the **DAHLET** ד for the **FAY** פ , like this: סֵדֶר , and the word becomes ＿＿＿＿＿＿＿ .

בְ   V

This letter בּ is called **BET**. This one בּ is called **VET** and has the saying sound of **V**.

The *name* of the Hebrew letter with the saying sound of **V** is _____ .

VAH   בַ

Read this line aloud, then copy the letter and vowel with the sound **BAY**:

בֵּ   בֵּ   בַּ   בֵּ ⬅ **start here**

Write your answer here: _____

SHAH

Read each syllable aloud, then copy the letter and vowel with the sound **SAY**:

שֵׁ   שַׁ   שֵׁ   שֵׁ ⬅

_____

3

Read each syllable aloud.

תַ תֵ תָ תֵ תֵ תֵ תָ תֵ ⬅

How many times did you read the letter and vowel **TAH**?

_____ times

VET ‫בּ‬ 1.
FAY ‫פ‬ 2.
TAHV ‫ת‬ 3.

You know two letters for each of the sounds below.

We'll write one; you do the other:

‫ח‬ CH _____

‫תּ‬ T _____

‫ו‬ V _____

KAH-DOSH,

KAH-DOSH,

KAH-DOSH

Here is the second letter we promised you:

This is TET ‫ט‬. You already know TAHV ‫תּ‬.

Place a ✓ under the new letter, TET.

‫תּ‬   ‫ט‬

◯   ◯

‫דִי‬   DEE

The name of this Hebrew letter ‫צ‬ is ‫צָדִי‬.

Write its name here: _____

FEH   ‫פֶ‬

To create the word for "BOOK" in Hebrew, we combine
‫סֵ‬, ‫פֶ‬, and RAYSH ‫ר‬, like this: ‫סֵפֶר‬.

The word for "BOOK" is _____ .

VET ב

This letter ב has no dot and is called **VET**.

Because the name of a Hebrew letter always starts with its saying sound, you know that **VET** has the saying sound of _____.

בֵּ BAY

Here are two more Hebrew letters. They look similar.

This one ר has the saying sound of **R**.

This one ד has the saying sound of **D**.

This letter, ד, has the saying sound of _____.

שַׁ SAY

How many times does **SHAY** appear in the line below?
Read each syllable aloud:

שַׁ שֵׁ שַׁ שֵׁ שֶׁ שַׁ ←

_____ times

6

Here are some letters you've learned. Under each one, write its saying sound:

TAHV	SHIN	RAYSH	BET
ת	שׁ	ר	בֵּ
____	____	____	____

PREE   פְּרִי

Let's review.

You've learned several pairs of letters in which one has a dot and the other does not. We'll write one; you write the other:

_____ _____ (1) BET   בּ

_____ _____ (2) PAY   פּ

_____ _____ (3) TAHV   תּ

KAH-DOSH

קָדוֹשׁ

"HOLY, HOLY, HOLY" is part of a prayer.

This is how it appears in Hebrew:

קָדוֹשׁ, קָדוֹשׁ, קָדוֹשׁ

"HOLY, HOLY, HOLY" is read:

_____, _____, _____

צִ   TSIH

Add the correct vowel to make this syllable DEE:

די

פֶ   SAY

When we add the vowel EH ֶ to the letter FAY פ, like this: פֶ, we read _____ .

V

The letter VET ‏ב‏ has the s_____
s_____ of **V.**

D

‏ר‏ has the saying sound of **R.**

‏ד‏ has the saying sound of **D.** The other letter, ‏ר‏, has the saying sound of _____ .

2

‏שׂ‏ has the sound _____ .

Now try these. Fill in the saying sounds:

‏ת‏ ‏שׂ‏ ‏ר‏ ‏ב‏

T SH R B

_____ TAHV   ‏ת‏

_____ DAHLET   ‏ד‏

_____ VET   ‏ב‏

_____ SIN   ‏שׂ‏

פְּ   P

You remember that when we combine the RAYSH ר with the vowel EE, like this: רִי, we read REE.

Add רִי to פְּ, פְּרִי, and the word is _____ as in BORAY _____ HAH-GAHFEN.

דוֹ   DO

קָ is read KAH.

דוֹ is read DO.

When we add the SHIN שׁ, like this: קָדוֹשׁ, we create the word that means "holy": קָדוֹשׁ.

The word for "holy" is read _____.

#5   צִי

Write the letter and vowel combination that reads TSIH:

_____

וֹס

#1 and #3

Here are the 2 letters with the saying sound of S, combined with vowels. Read them aloud, then copy the syllable that reads SAY:

שֵׂ   סָ   שְׂ   שֵׂ   סָ   שֵׂ ←

Write it here: _____

saying sound

The name of this letter ב, with the saying sound of **V**, is _____ .

R

The Hebrew letter with the saying sound of **D** is written _____ .

SHAH שַׁ

There are two ways to write the letter and vowel that make the sound **SAH**.

Write them here: _____ or _____

T
D
V
S

ת
ד
ב
שׁ

Did you remember that the name of each letter starts with its saying sound?

Check one: Yes _____   No _____

1 & 6

The vowel **SH'VAH** ְ has no sound.

Added to the letter פ, we read this syllable פְּ as _____ .

קָ   **KAH**

You know that this syllable קוֹ reads **KO**.

Add the vowel **O** as in **TORAH** to make the letter below read **DO**:

ד

7

One of the sounds below reads **TSO**.
Which number?

Read each sound aloud:

צִי   צֲו   צֶ   צֵ   צָ   צֵו   צֶ   צֵ   ←
(8)   (7)   (6)   (5)   (4)   (3)   (2)   (1)

#_____

4

We've placed the vowel **O** וֹ as in **TORAH** before each ט and ם below.

Which numbers read **OM**?

טוֹ   טוֹ   םוֹ   טוֹ   םוֹ
(5)   (4)   (3)   (2)   (1)

#_____ and #_____

VET   בְ

How many times does **VET** appear below?

בֿ   בֿ   בְ   בֿ   בֿ   בְ   בֿ   ב

_____ times

דָ

How many letters with the saying sound
of **D** appear on the line below?

ד   ד   ד   ד   ב   ד   ב   ד   ד   ד   ד   ד

_____

שֻׁ
and
שָׁ   SAH

Put the three vowels you know under the letters below to
make the correct sounds:

SHAH   SAH   SHAY

שׁ   שׁ   שׁ

If "Yes," go on to the
next frame.

If "No," start again at

Lesson 4: Frame 16.

The vowel ⸱⸱ has the sound **AY** as in **DAY**.

Read each syllable aloud, then copy the letter and vowel
with the sound **TAY**:

שׁ   בֵ   תֵּ   דֵ   ⬅

_____

פִ FIH

Two sounds below read **PAY**. Which numbers are they?

Read each sound aloud:

בֵּ בֶּ בֵּ בֶּ בֵּ בֶ בֵּ פֵּ ←

8   7   6   5   4   3   2   1

Write the numbers here: _____ _____

כֹּ קוֹ

#1 and **#4**

Remember these letters?

ד   שׁ   כ

DAHLET   SHIN   CHAHF

Read the letters and vowels below. Copy the syllable with the sound **KAH**:

קוֹ   קַ   בֵ   שַׁ ←

_____

צִי TSEE

BET ב is often mistaken for **KAHF** כ.

DAHLET ד is often mistaken for **RAYSH** ר.

Here's another set to watch out for:

AHYIN ע and **TSAHDEE** צ

Draw a circle around each **AHYIN**:

ע ע צ ע ע ע ע צ ע צ צ ע

How many circles did you draw? _____

ס SAHMECH

ם FINAL MEM

How many **SAHMECH**s do you count in this row?

ס ם ס ם ס ם

_____

4

It is easy to tell the difference between **VET** and **BET** because only one of these letters has a dot in the middle.

Which letter has the dot?

_____

5

Let's practice writing the letter with the saying sound of **R**:

____ ____ ____ ____ ר ⬅ **start here**

Let's review:

SHAH   SAH   SHAY

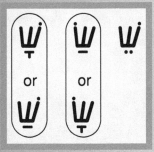

ר   ד   בּ   ב

RAYSH   DAHLET   BET   VET

Write the letter with the saying sound of **B**: _____

Write the letter with the saying sound of **D**: _____

Write the letter with the saying sound of **R**: _____

Write the letter with the saying sound of **V**: _____

תּ   TAY

TAY can be written two ways.

Write them here:

_____   ת

פֶ

PEH

Write the sound **FIH**: _____

2

The sound KO appears twice below.
Which numbers are they?

כִּי   קוֹ   קֶ   קַ   כוֹ
(5)   (4)   (3)   (2)   (1)

_____ and # _____

TSAH

צ

Helpful hints:

יEE   IH   וֹO   וOO   AY   EH   SILENT   U

Copy the TSAHDEE צ and vowel combination in the
line below that reads **TSEE**:

צ   צִי   צֶ   צָ   צְ   צוֹ

_____

end

In the circle, write the **SAHMECH**: ◯

In the square, write the **FINAL MEM**: ☐

BET ב

ב has the saying sound of _____ and is called _____.

בּ has the saying sound of _____ and is called _____.

ר ד ד

ד has the saying sound of _____, and ר has the saying sound of _____.

בּ = B
ד = D
ר = R
ב = V

בּ is called _____; its saying sound is _____.

ר is called _____; its saying sound is _____.

ב is called _____; its saying sound is _____.

תָּ תֳּ
or
תָּ תֳּ

You know that ַ and ָ are the vowels AH as in OOMPAH.

Read these syllables aloud, then put a ☐ around the one that has the sound DAH.

דָ   תַ   שַׁ   בָּ ←

פ פ פ

Did you remember the dot in **PAY**?

Read each syllable aloud, then copy the letter and vowel with the sound **PEH**.

Helpful hints:

SILENT AY OO וּ IH EH AH AH Oוֹ

פ   פ   פ   פ   פ   פ ⟵

_____

קַ **KAH**

Helpful hints:

AY AH EH 'EE U Oוֹ OOוּ SILENT

Read the line below aloud.

How many times did you read **KEH**?

קַ   קוּ   קֶ   קַ   קֶ   קֶ ⟵

_____ times

צ צ צ

When we combine the **TSAHDEE** צ and the vowel **AH** ַ, we create this syllable צַ, read **TSAH**.

So this syllable צַ is read _____ .

ס

SAHMECH

The **SAHMECH** ס may appear at the beginning of a word, in the middle of a word, or at the end of a word.

The **FINAL MEM** ם may be used only at the

_____ of a word.

B; BET ‎בּ
V; VET ‎ב

In addition to letters, Hebrew has vowels that usually appear below letters. Vowels are symbols that tell you what sounds to add to letters. This vowel _____ has the sound AY as in DAY.

What is the sound of the vowel that has two dots side by side?

_____ as in _____

D

R

The name of this letter ‎ר is RAYSH.

This one ‎ד is called DAHLET and has the saying sound of D.

The name of the Hebrew letter with the saying sound of R is R __ __ __ __ .

BET; B ‎בּ
RAYSH; R ‎ר
VET; V ‎ב

The name of ‎שׁ is _____; its saying sound is _____.

The name of ‎ר is _____; its saying sound is _____.

The name of ‎שׁ is _____; its saying sound is _____.

‎דָ DAH

Read each syllable aloud, then copy the one that has the sound BAH:

‎שַׁ   ‎בֵּ   ‎רֵ   ‎בֵּ   ‎חָ   ←

_____

ף ף ף

And this is how to write the **PAY**:

ף step 3   ף step 2   כ step 1

Now you:

___ ___ ___ ___ ף

KIH   קִ

When we add the vowel **AH** ‑ to כ, like this: כָ, we read **KAH**.

Write **KAH** another way with the same vowel: _____

TSAHDEE   צ

Let's practice writing the **TSAHDEE** צ:

צ step 3   ⅃ step 2   \ step 1

Now you try:

___ ___ ___ ___ צ

SAHMECH
S
ס

SAHMECH ס looks very much like the **FINAL MEM** ם.

Circle the **SAHMECH**:   ם   ס

AY as in DAY ⠤

Write the Hebrew vowel that has the sound AY as in DAY.
Don't forget to put it under the line. _____

RAYSH ר

RAYSH ר has the saying sound of R.

DAHLET ד has the saying sound of _____.

SHIN; SH שׁ

DAHLET; D דָ

SIN; S שׂ

Each of these letters is combined with one of the AH
vowels. Read each syllable aloud. Then copy the letter and
vowel with the sound RAH:

שַׂ דָ בָּ בַ דָ שַׁ ←

_____

בָּ BAH

Two of these syllables have the sound TAY. Which are they?

תֵּ שַׁ דָ תֶ תֵ בֵּ
(6) (5) (4) (3) (2) (1)

_____ and # _____

FAY; F   פ

PAY; P   פ

This is how to write the **FAY**:

פ step 2   כ step 1

Now you try:

____   ____   ____   פ

K

IH

We put the vowel **.** to the *right* of the downstroke.

The sound of this letter and vowel 7 is

_____ .

TS as in **CATS**

This letter **צ**, with the saying sound of **TS**, is called

_____ .

SAHMECH   ס

This letter **ס**, called _____ , has the saying

sound of _____ .

___
..   AY

AY .. is not a letter. It is a vowel, and it is written
_____ the line.

D

This letter ⊤ has the saying sound of _____ and is
called __ __ __ __ __ __ .

רַ   RAH

Each letter below is combined with the vowel AY .. as in DAY.

Read each syllable aloud, then circle the one that reads BAY:

בֵּ   שֵׁ   בֵּ   רֵ   שֵׁ   רֵ ←

#3
and
6

חֵ

חֵ

Helpful hints: .. = AY

_ or ָ = AH

Put the correct vowel under each letter to complete
each syllable:

VAY   SHAY   RAH

בֵ   שֵׁ   ר

5

פ is called _____ and has the saying sound of _____ .

פ is called _____ and has the saying sound of _____ .

ק ק ק

KOOF ק has the saying sound of _____ .

Remember ִ ? It has the sound _____ as in **TICK**.

TSAHDEE צ

TSAHDEE צ has the saying sound of _____ as in _____ .

ט ט ט

The name of this letter ט, with the saying sound of S,

is _____ .

under

What is the sound of ָ◌ ?

_____ as in _____

D

DAHLET

ר is **RAYSH** and has the saying sound of _____ .

בֵ

BAY

Now read each of the following syllables aloud. Put a ☐ around the one that reads **SHAH**:

רָ   בֵ   שַ   שֵ   בֵ   רַ

VAY SHAY RAH

בֵ   שַ   רַ

or

רָ

This time we'll provide the vowels. Put the correct letter over each vowel to complete each syllable:

SAH   BAY   DAY

_   ..   ..

F

How many times does the letter **FAY** appear below?

9 9 9 9 9 9 9 9 9 9 9

_____ times

K

Let's practice writing **KOOF** ק :

ק step 3   ٦ step 2   ‒ step 1

Now you:

___ ___ ___ ___ ק

TS

The letter ץ, with the saying sound of **TS** as in **CATS**, is called **TSAHDEE**.

The name of this letter ץ is **TS**_____.

S

This is the way to write **SAHMECH** ס :

ס step 2   ‒ step 1

Now you try:

___ ___ ___ ___ ס

AY as in DAY ..

In Hebrew, we write most letters *on* the line and most vowels *below* the line. Let's write בּ, with the saying sound of B, and AY .. as in DAY. We get בֵּ, a syllable that we read as BAY.

How do we read בֵּ? _____

R

The vowel _ has the sound AH as in OOMPAH.

Placed under the RAYSH ר, you get רַ.

The sound of רַ is _____.

SHAH

Ready for something more difficult?

Write the correct sound under each letter and vowel. We'll do the first one:

בַּ   שַׁ   בֵּ   רַ

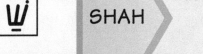

4	3	2	RAH
			1

Read each line aloud. Place a ✓ next to the one that reads DAY BAT SHAH:

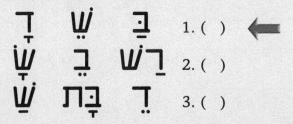

רָ   שַׁ   בַּ   1. ( ) ⬅

שַׁ   בֵּ   רְ   2. ( )

שַׁ   תַּ   דֵּ   3. ( )

שַׁ בֵּ דָ

SAH BAY DAY

P

Since פ is called **PAY**, it shouldn't be a surprise that פ is called **FAY** and has the saying sound of _____ .

כ   KAHF

The saying sound of both **KOOF** ק and **KAHF** כ is _____ .

1. TET
2. CHET
3. GIMMEL

ט ח ג

This is a new letter צ. It has an unusual sound—**TS** as in **CATS**.

The saying sound of צ is _____ as in **CATS**.

SAHMECH   ס

SAHMECH ס is the other Hebrew letter with the saying sound of _____ .

VAY   בֵ

Read each sound aloud, then copy the letter and vowel with the sound **VAY**:

בֵ   בֵ   בֵ   בֵ   ⬅ **start here**

_____

RAH   דַ

Let's try it again:

The vowel _ also has the sound **AH** as in **OOMPAH**.

Placed under the **DAHLET** ד, you get דַ.

The sound of דַ is _____ .

1. RAH
2. BAY
3. SAY
4. VAH

דַ
בֵ
שֵׁ
דַ

Now let's build a word:

This syllable דַ reads _____ .

line 3

Ready to build a word . . . one you may already know?

When we add the vowel **AH** to the שׁ, like this שַׁ, we read **SAH**.

But this syllable שׁ is _____ .

P

This letter ‫פ‬ is called **PAY** and has the saying sound of _____ .

KOOF   ‫ק‬

This is **KOOF**: ‫ק‬

This is **KAHF**: _____

KAHF   ‫כ‬
PAY   ‫פ‬
BET   ‫ב‬

Here are pairs of letters that are often mistaken for one another. We'll write the name of the first letter in each group; you write the other:

1. _____ ‫ט‬   MEM ‫מ‬

2. _____ ‫ח‬   HAY ‫ה‬

3. _____ ‫ג‬   NUN ‫נ‬

V
CH
no

Guess what?

The Hebrew saying sound **S** is also written 2 ways.

Which is the new letter with the saying sound of **S**?

‫ס‬   ‫ש‬

SAHMECH   SIN

Write its name here: _____

בַ VAY

You remember, of course, that we read Hebrew from right to left.

Let's practice reading aloud the Hebrew way:

בֵ בֵ בֵ בֵ בֵ ← **start here**

Now go back and count how many times you read **BAY**.

_____ times

DAH דָ

You're doing great! Now try this.

Under each letter, write its saying sound:

DAHLET   BET   VET   RAYSH

ד   בּ   ב   ר   ← **start here**

___ 4.   ___ 3.   ___ 2.   ___ 1.

RAH רַ

Add **VET** ב to ר, and you have the Hebrew word for Rabbi: רַבּ.

Write its sound here: _____

SHAH שַׁ

Add the correct vowel to make this syllable read **BAHT**:

בת

F

The Hebrew letter with the saying sound of **F** is written **פ**.

This letter **פ**, with the dot, has the saying sound of _____ .

below

ק is not a final letter, though it *is* written partly below the line. **ק** is called _____ .

1. N

2. CH

3. M

ן
ך
ם

Look at Column I, then add a dot to the middle of each letter in Column II and write its name:

II		I	
_____	כ	CHAHF	כ
_____	פ	FAY	פ
_____	ב	VET	ב

(1) TS

(2) Z

(3) TS

צ
ז
צ

You remember that there are several pairs of letters in the Hebrew alphabet with the same saying sound.

VET **ב** and VAHV **ו** have the saying sound of _____ .

CHAHF **כ** and CHET **ח** have the saying sound of _____ .

AHLEF **א** and AHYIN **ע** have _____ sound.

2

Read each line aloud. Place a ✔ next to the line that reads
VAY VAY BAY:

בַ בַ בַ 1. ( ) ← **start here**

בֵ בֵ בֵ 2. ( )

בֵ בֵ בֵ 3. ( )

ד ב ב ר

D B V R

Ready to read your first Hebrew word?

בַּד

Write its sound here: _____

RAHV בַּר

(That was easy, wasn't it?)

Here's another word. This time it's the name of a letter you've learned.

Here's the word: רֵשׁ

Write its sound here: _____

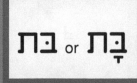

בַת or בָת

BAHT

We'll combine שׁ with בָת to form the Hebrew word for Sabbath, שַׁבָּת.

Write the word here: _____

Check your answer here:

F

פ has the saying sound of **P**.

Without the dot, it has the saying sound of _____ .

Check your answer here:

KOOF ק

KOOF ק is a regular Hebrew **K**, just like KAHF כּ.

It is *not* a final letter, even though it is written partly _____ the line.

Check your answer here:

1. V
2. T
3. silent

Under each of these **FINAL LETTERS**, write its saying sound:

FINAL MEM   FINAL CHAHF   FINAL NUN

ם   ך   ן

3. _____   2. _____   1. _____

Check your answer here:

TSAHDEE   צ

FINAL TSAHDEE   ץ

ZAHYIN   ז

Under each letter, write its saying sound:

צ   ז   ץ

_____   _____   _____
(3)   (2)   (1)

line 3

Congratulations—you have just finished Lesson 1!
You have learned that:

BET בּ has the saying sound of B.

VET ב has the saying sound of V.

.. is the vowel AY as in DAY.

TURN BACK TO PAGE 3 TO BEGIN LESSON 2.

BAHR

You may recognize the common spelling of this word—BAR—as in BAR MITZVAH.*

You've completed Lesson 2!
You have learned that:

RAYSH ר has the saying sound of R.

DAHLET ד has the saying sound of D.

_ and ָ are vowels that make the sound AH as in OOMPAH.

*We'll introduce the common English spellings of certain Hebrew words. Please use these common spellings in your written answers.

TURN BACK TO PAGE 3 TO BEGIN LESSON 3.

RAYSH   רֵשׁ

You've completed Lesson 3! You have learned that SHIN שׁ has the saying sound of SH and that SIN שׂ has the saying sound of S.

TURN BACK TO PAGE 3 TO BEGIN LESSON 4.

שַׁבָּת

SHAH-BAHT
(commonly spelled SHABBAT)

You've completed Lesson 4!
You have learned that

ת is TAHV, that

תּ is TAHV, and that even though one has a dot and the other has none, both have the same saying sound.

TURN TO THE NEXT PAGE TO CONTINUE.

Lesson 13: Frame 1

Begin Lesson 13 Here

Remember how CHAHF כ becomes KAHF כּ when we add a dot?

Here's the last Hebrew letter that makes that change:

פּ has the saying sound of F.

פּ has the saying sound of P.

The letter that has no dot is written פ and has the saying sound of _____ .

TURN THE PAGE TO CHECK YOUR ANSWER.

Lesson 14: Frame 1

Begin Lesson 14 Here

You're going to learn 2 new letters in this lesson. Each one sounds like a letter you already know.

The first one is KOOF ק . It has the saying sound of K. It dips partly below the line.

The name of ק is _____ .

TURN THE PAGE TO CHECK YOUR ANSWER.

Lesson 15: Frame 1

Begin Lesson 15 Here

General review:

Each pair of letters below has the same saying sound.

Next to each pair, write the saying sound:

1. _____ ו ב

2. _____ ח כּ

3. _____ ע א

TURN THE PAGE TO CHECK YOUR ANSWER.

Lesson 16: Frame 1

Begin Lesson 16 Here

These are the newest letters you have learned:

צ is read TS. It is called _____ .

ץ is read TS. It is called _____ _____ .

ז is read Z. It is called _____ .

TURN THE PAGE TO CHECK YOUR ANSWER.

Congratulations!

This is the middle page.
You have now finished four lessons.
Lessons 5, 6, 7, and 8 begin on
the next page.

Congratulations!

This is the middle page. You have now
finished twelve lessons.
Lessons 13, 14, 15, and 16 begin on
the next page.

Begin Lesson 5 Here

Which one of the letters below have we not yet studied in these lessons?

בּ   תּ   מ   שׁ   ר

VET   TAHV   MEM   SIN   RAYSH

Write its name here: _____

TURN THE PAGE TO CHECK YOUR ANSWER.

Begin Lesson 6 Here

Hebrew has no capital letters, not even to start a sentence. But it does have 5 letters that are written differently when they *end* a word.

There are 5 Hebrew letters that are written differently when they appear at the _____ of a word.

TURN THE PAGE TO CHECK YOUR ANSWER.

Begin Lesson 7 Here

In the last lesson, you learned two vowels: O וֹ as in TORAH and OO וּ as in FOOD.

Now we are going to learn a new letter.

This one may look familiar—it's ו *without* a dot.

When you see ו without a dot, it is a regular letter—called VAHV. Write the letter VAHV ו here: _____

TURN THE PAGE TO CHECK YOUR ANSWER.

Begin Lesson 8 Here

In lesson 7, you learned 3 new letters:

YUD י   VAHV ו   FINAL NUN ן

The only letter of these 3 that we write *on* the line is

_____.

TURN THE PAGE TO CHECK YOUR ANSWER.

C

You've learned that GIMMEL **ג** has the saying sound of G as in GO, and that NUN **נ** has the saying sound of N.

You've made great progress! Keep it up!

TURN BACK TO PAGE 66 TO BEGIN LESSON 10.

אֶחָד

EH-CHAHD

Great job! You've learned that **ֶ** is the vowel EH, that CHET **ח** has the saying sound of CH, and that HAY **ה** has the saying sound of H.

TURN BACK TO PAGE 66 TO BEGIN LESSON 11.

CHAH

CH

כָ

כְ

You're ready for Lesson 12! You've learned that CHAHF **כ** has the saying sound of CH, that KAHF **כּ** has the saying sound of K, and that FINAL CHAHF **ך** appears only at the end of a word.

TURN BACK TO PAGE 66 TO BEGIN LESSON 12.

SH'MA YISRAEL

ADONAI

Great job—you read part of the SH'MA!

In Lesson 12, you learned that the vowel **.** has the sound IH as in TICK, and **ִי** has the sound EE.

On to Lesson 13!

TURN TO THE NEXT PAGE TO CONTINUE

Check your answer here:

MEM מ

This is MEM: מ. The first letter of its name is M, so מ has the saying sound of _____.

Check your answer here:

end

The 5 Hebrew letters that we write differently at the end of a word are called **FINAL LETTERS**.

Hebrew has how many **FINAL LETTERS**? _____

Check your answer here:

ו VAHV

This ו is the *letter* **VAHV**.

Put a dot over it וֹ, and it becomes the *vowel* **O** as in **TORAH**.

Put a dot in the middle וּ, and it becomes the vowel **OO** as in **FOOD**.

Standing alone, this ו is the letter _____.

Check your answer here:

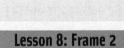

One letter in the Hebrew alphabet does not reach down to the bottom line; it is the **YUD**.

YUD is written like this: _____.

GAHM גַּם

One of the words below reads **NAYR**. Which one?

(C)   (B)   (A)

נֵר   גַּן   גַּם

Answer: (   )

חַ or חָ חֶ

CHAY HAH CHEH

You know that **AHLEF** א has no sound and that **DAHLET** ד has the sound **D**.

Here are the letters in the word **EH-CHAHD**. You fill in the vowels to make it read **EH-CHAHD**. Use this **AH** ָ vowel.

אחד

CHAH חַ

This **FINAL** letter and vowel combination חַ is read _____.

This **FINAL** letter and vowel combination חַ is read _____.

שְׁמַע

SH'MA

You know how to read **SH'MA** שְׁמַע.

And you remember **YISRAEL** יִשְׂרָאֵל.

Can you recognize this phrase from our most important prayer?

שְׁמַע יִשְׂרָאֵל יְיָ

Write it here: _____ _____ _____

M

מ has the saying sound of **M** and is called _____ .

5

The 5 special Hebrew letters that appear at the end of a word are called _____ **LETTERS**.

VAHV   ו

The saying sound of **VAHV** is **V**, and it is written _____ .
(Remember **VET** ב , the other Hebrew letter with the saying sound of **V**?)

י   YUD

This ו is one of several letters that are written partly *below* the line.

This letter ו is called _____ _____ .

נֵר NAYR

We read גָּן as GAHN.

We read גַּם as _____ .

חוֹ CHO

To complete each syllable, place the correct *vowel* under each letter. We'll do the first one:

חַ   ה   חֶ

CHAY   HAH   CHEH

LAHCH לָךְ

You remember that this vowel ָ is read AH.

Sometimes the vowel ָ is added to the FINAL CHAHF ךְ, like this: ךָ.

This letter ך with the AH ָ added is ךָ and is read

_____ .

MAH מַ

In Lesson 8, we learned the word SH'MA.

Here are the letters in the word SH'MA; you fill in the correct vowels:

שמע

MEM   מ

MEM מ has the saying sound of _____ , and ָ has the sound of _____ as in OOMPAH.

FINAL

The 5 **FINAL LETTERS** appear only at the _____ of a word.

ו   VAHV

ו is called **VAHV** and has the saying sound of _____ .

FINAL NUN   ן

Let's review some letters you've learned:

ל   ת   שׂ   ד

LAHMED   TAHV   SIN   DAHLET

Write the letter with the saying sound of S: _____

Write the letter with the saying sound of L: _____

Write the letter with the saying sound of T: _____

Write the letter with the saying sound of D: _____

NAYR נֵר

Can you write the Hebrew word for candle?

_____

7

Reminder:　　AY וֹ　oo וּ
　　　　　　　ֵ

Remember the difference between CHET ח and HAY ה?

חוּ הוֹ חוֹ חֶ הוֹ

Copy the letter and vowel with the sound CHO:

_____

CH

This vowel ְ is the SH'VAH, and it has no sound.

When we add the SH'VAH to the FINAL CHAHF like this: ךְ, we simply read CH.

Therefore, when we see ךְ at the end of לְךְ, we read the word as LAH_____.

SH שִׁ

Remember how we read the syllable when the ַ appears below the MEM מ?

This syllable מַ reads _____.

M
AH

The sound of this letter and vowel מַ is —————.

end

In this lesson, you will learn one of these **FINAL LETTERS**.

This is the regular **MEM** מ.

This is the **FINAL MEM** ם. It is called **FINAL MEM** because it is the form used only at the ——————— of a word.

V

This letter ו is called ——————— and has the saying sound of ———————.

 שׁ   S
ל   L
 תּ   T
ד   D

Fill in the saying sounds for the following letters:

—————— VET   ב

—————— RAYSH   ר

—————— TAHV   ת

—————— MEM   מ

נֵר   NAYR

נֵר, the Hebrew word for candle, is written **NUN**, **AY** as in **DAY**, and **RAYSH**.

So נֵר has the sound _____ .

ח   ה

CHET   **HAY**
(2)   **(1)**

Draw a circle around each **HAY** below:

ה   ה   ח   ה   ח   ה   ה   ה   ה   ה

How many did you circle? _____

FINAL CHAHF ך

FINAL CHAHF ך has the saying sound of _____ .

ADONAI   יי
        ָ:

This is **AHYIN** ע, and it has no sound.

This is the **SILENT VOWEL SH'VAH** : , and it has no sound.

Here we've added the : to the **SHIN** שְׁ .

Its sound is _____ .

MAH מָ

You remember that ָ also has the sound **AH** as in

_____, and ֵ has the sound **AY** as in _____.

end

MEM is written this way מ.

When you see the letter that looks like a square at the end of a word ם, you know it is **FINAL** _____.

VAHV
V
ו

Put a ✓ over each **VAHV**:

ו ו ו ו ו ו ן

How many ✓'s do you have? _____

V	VET	ב
R	RAYSH	ר
T	TAHV	ת
M	MEM	מ

Now for something new and different: Hebrew has 2 letters that have no sound. Then why are they there?

We believe that once, many years ago, they *did* have a sound, but now they do not.

Hebrew has how many silent letters? _____

GIMMEL ✓   ג

AH ✓   -

FINAL NUN ✓   ן

Here's another Hebrew word: NAYR is the word for candle.

Below are the NUN נ and RAYSH ר. Fill in the correct vowel to make the word NAYR:

נר

H

Write the names of these letters:

ח   ה

_____   _____

(2)   (1)

end

ך has the saying sound of CH and is called

F_____ CH_____.

ADONAI   יְיָ

Even though you may think to sound out the letters of יְיָ, you know that יְיָ is always read:

_____

OOMPAH DAY

Put an **X** over each syllable in the line below with the sound **MAY**:

מָ מֶ מַ מֵ מֶ

Number of **X**'s: _____

FINAL MEM ם

LAHMED ל begins above the line. Most vowels, such as AH ַ as in OOMPAH, are written below the line.

But both MEM מ and _____ ם are written *on* the line.
(name of letter)

4

When ו stands alone, it is the letter _____.

2

The **SILENT LETTERS** look like this: ע א

Neither this letter א nor this letter ע has a saying sound. Both are S_____ L_____.

GAHN   גָן

To write the word גָן, we used two letters and one vowel.
Place a ✔ next to the ones we used:

GIMMEL ◯   YUD ◯   OO ◯

O ◯   AH ◯   FINAL NUN ◯

CHET   ח

The saying sound of ח is CH.

The saying sound of ח is _____.

CH

The **FINAL CHAHF** is written ___ך___ and appears only
at the _____ of a word.

LORD

Instead of God's name, you often see יְיָ in Hebrew.

יְיָ is never sounded. When we see יְיָ, we always read

_____ .

3

Read each sound aloud, then circle the one that has the sound MAH:

← מֶ תָ רְ מַ בְ

FINAL MEM ם

MEM looks a little like a house with a chimney.

FINAL MEM looks a little like a square. How many times does the regular letter MEM appear here?

ם מ ם מ ם ם מ ם

———— times

VAHV ו

Change the letter VAHV to the vowel O as in TORAH:

ו

SILENT LETTERS

This letter א is called AHLEF.

While the letter א has no saying sound, it *does* have a name. The name of this letter א is ——————.

GAHM גַּם

You know that when you add the FINAL MEM ם to גַּ, you create the word GAHM גַּם.

Now we'll change one letter to make another word. This time we'll add the FINAL NUN ן to גַּ, like this: גַּן.

Now we have the word _____ .

HAY ח

This letter ח is called HAY.

This letter ח is called _____ .

כֹּ or כֹ

בֶּ   כְּ   כָּ
BAY   CH   KAH

You know that the CHAHF is written כ.

The FINAL CHAHF is written ך and appears only at the end of a word.

The FINAL CHAHF ך has the saying sound of _____ .

ADONAI יְיָ

People have said ADONAI to signify God's name for more than 2000 years.

When we see יְיָ and say ADONAI, we know ADONAI means _____ .

מַ MAH

If your answer was incorrect, go back to Lesson 5: Frame 1 for review.

Ready to write **MEM**? This one's a little tricky!

מ step 3   מ step 2   ∩ step 1

You try: _____ _____ _____ מ_____

3

The **FINAL MEM** is written like this: **▢**, and has the saying sound of _____.

וֹ   *O* as in **TORAH**

The vowel *OO* as in **FOOD** has the dot in the _____, like this: וֹ.

AHLEF   א

The name of this letter ﬠ is AHYIN. Both AHYIN ﬠ and AHLEF א are SILENT LETTERS. AHYIN ﬠ and AHLEF א have names, but they do not have S_____G S_____DS.

GAH   ג

To create the Hebrew word "also," we add the **FINAL MEM** ם to גַ, like this: גַם.

We now have the word _____ .

H

ח has the saying sound of **H** and is called _____ .

#4   בְ

To complete each syllable, place the correct *vowel* under each letter:

בֵ   בְ   בַ

BAY   CH   KAH

EE   יִ

YUD י has another important role.

Instead of writing God's name, the Hebrew is יְיָ. This word is **NEVER READ.**

When we see יְיָ, we say **AH-DO-NAI** (commonly spelled **ADONAI**), which means **LORD.**

So, when you see יְיָ, you read _____ NAI.

מ מ מ

In the blank space below, copy the letter and vowel combination that has the sound MAY:

מֶ מָ מַ

_____

M

This letter מ is called _____.

And ם is called _____ _____.

middle

How many vowels below have the sound O as in TORAH? Read the line aloud:

וֹ וֹ וּ וֹ וּ וֹ וּ וֹ וּ וֹ וֹ וֹ ←

Write the number here: _____

SAYING SOUNDS

Here are the two SILENT LETTERS, which have no saying sounds. Draw a circle around the AHLEF:

א ע

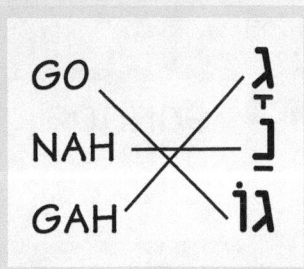

When we combine the GIMMEL ג and the vowel ָ , we have the sound GAH גָ .

Read this syllable: גָ

Write its sound here: _____

ה   HAY

The name of the letter ה is HAY.

Since the first sound in the name of each Hebrew letter is its saying sound, you know that the saying sound of HAY ה is _____ .

ב   BET

Our vowels:

OO וּ   O וֹ   AY ֵ   EH ֶ   AH ָ   AH ַ   SILENT ְ

Only one letter and vowel combination below reads CH. Which one?

בוּ   כֶ   כָ   חַ   בוֹ
(5)   (4)   (3)   (2)   (1)

Answer: (   )

יִשְׂרָאֵל

YIHS-RAH-AYL
(commonly spelled
YISRAEL)

If you read this correctly, continue on. If your answer was incorrect, go back to Lesson 12: Frame 16 for review.

You know YUD and IH יִ form the first syllable in the word YISRAEL יִשְׂרָאֵל .

But when the י comes *after* the ִ , in this way ִי , we read it as _____ .

מֵ MAY

You're doing so well that we're ready to learn a new letter.

MEM = מ RAYSH = ר
TAHV = ת LAHMED = ל

Which letter is new? L ____________

MEM מ
FINAL MEM ם

Let's practice writing FINAL MEM:

ם step 2 ר step 1

____ ____ ____ ם

6

Remember these? ֵ = AY as in DAY
ַ = AH as in OOMPAH
ָ = AH as in OOMPAH

Add the correct vowel to the VAHV ו below so that it reads VAY: ו

(א) AHLEF

If you were incorrect, go back to Lesson 8: Frame 6 and review the lesson.

Do you sound this letter AHLEF א?

Check the correct box:

Yes ☐ No ☐

3

Helpful hints:

AH AH AY O וֹ OO וּ SILENT

$\underset{\tau}{}$ $\underset{-}{}$ $\underset{\because}{}$ וֹ וּ $\underset{:}{}$

Draw a line to connect each matching set:

GO   גְ

NAH   גָ

GAH   גוֹ

5

There is another letter that looks very much like
CHET ח: the letter HAY ה.

The HAY is not attached here ↱ה.

The letter HAY is written _____.

ח   כ

CHET   CHAHF
(2)   (1)

HAY   KAHF
(4)   (3)

ה   כּ

Just as VET ב and CHAHF כ can be mistaken for one
another, so can BET בּ and KAHF כּ.

KAHF is written כּ. This is BET: _____

רָ   RAH

You might have used ַ,
but in this word we use ָ.

Ready for the word?

יִשְ is read YIHS. We'll add two more syllables, רָ and

אֵל, like this: יִשְׂרָאֵל.

The word is _____.

LAHMED ל

The **LAHMED** ל begins with **L**. Therefore, its saying sound is _____.

□ □ □

Draw a **MEM** in this space:

Now draw a **FINAL MEM** in this space:

וָ VAY

You know that ָ is the vowel **AH** as in **OOMPAH**.

Added to the letter **VAHV** וָ, it reads

_____.

✓NO

Let's practice writing the **SILENT LETTER AHLEF**:

א step 3   ע step 2   \ step 1

It's a bit tricky, so do it slowly:

___ ___ ___ א

6

Draw a circle around each syllable that reads GAY:

נֵ גֵ נֵ גֵ גֵ נֵ

How many circles? _____

CHEH חֶ

Read each syllable below aloud.

How many times does the sound CHAH appear?

חָ חֱ חֵ חַ חֶ חָ חָ חֵ חַ ←

_____ times

3

כחכ

Under each letter, write its name:

ה   כּ   ח   כ

_____ _____ _____ _____
(4)   (3)   (2)   (1)

YIHS יְשׁ

Write the letter and vowel combination that
reads RAH: _____

L

This letter **ל** has the saying sound of L and is called

_____ .

מ MEM

ם FINAL MEM

ם has the saying sound of _____

and is called _____ _____ .

VAH

וָ

Now we can write the name of the letter **ו** in Hebrew.

It is **וָו**, which has the sound _____ .

א א א

We know that the AHLEF has no saying sound.

When we combine the AHLEF **א** with the vowel AY **..**
as in DAY, like this: **אֵ**, the sound remains AY.

The syllable **אֵ** is read _____ .

Here are the letters **GIMMEL** and **NUN**.

G ג

N נ

How many times does the letter **NUN** appear below?

נ ג נ נ נ ג ג נ נ נ

_____ times

ח ח ח

AH   AH   EH   AY

ָ   ַ   ֶ   ֵ

חַ has the sound **CHAH**.

חֵ has the sound _____.

CH כ

K כ

Draw a circle around each letter below with the saying sound of **CH**. Remember: ה is **HAY**, not **CHET**.

כ כ ה ח כ

How many letters did you circle? _____

אֵל

AYL

The syllable יֶשׁ reads _____.

LAHMED ל

When you see ל, you know that it is called

_____ and has the saying sound of _____.

M

FINAL MEM ם

There are 2 vowels that are not written below the line.

One of these vowels appears in this group. Find it:

‥   וֹ   -   ָ

Write the new vowel here: _____

VAHV וָו

Three of the sounds below read VAH.

Which ones?

וְ   וָ   וְ   וַ   וָ   וְ
6   5   4   3   2   1

_____   # _____   # _____

AH אַ

Let's try another one. We'll combine א with the vowel O
וֹ as in TORAH: אוֹ. We read this syllable as O.

The א, combined with the vowel וֹ, like this: אוֹ,

is read _____.

ג GIMMEL

Next to each letter, write its saying sound:

_____ ג

_____ נ

CH

Let's practice writing the letter **CHET**:

ח step 2   ר step 1

Now you try:

___ ___ ___ ___ ח

4

בּ has the saying sound of _____.

ב has the saying sound of _____.

#4   אֵ

Place the vowel **..** under the correct letter to make this syllable read AYL: אל

LAHMED L	ל

Notice that we write all letters except one completely between the lines. Which is the one letter that begins *above* the line?

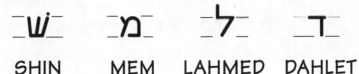

SHIN　　MEM　　LAHMED　　DAHLET

_____

וֹ

Here is the vowel you just wrote: וֹ

Notice the dot *on top*. This vowel וֹ has the sound O as in TORAH.

The vowel O וֹ as in TORAH has a dot on _____.

וֹ וֹ וֹ

#5　3　2

Now we are going to learn the smallest Hebrew letter.

Its name is YUD, and it is written י.

The first letter of YUD is _____; this is its saying sound.

OO	אֹל

Ready for something more challenging? This ל is the LAHMED.

You add the correct vowel to make this word read AHL:

אל

גֹ   G

Here is the letter NUN נ.

Write the letter GIMMEL: ＿＿＿

CHET   ח

ח is the letter CHET. It has the saying sound of ＿＿＿＿＿＿.

כּ   KAHF

Did you remember the dot?

How many times does KAHF כּ appear below?

כּ   כ   כּ   כ   כּ   כ

＿＿＿ times

LEE   לִי

Let's build a long word—one you may know well.

One of these syllables reads AY. Which one?

דָ   אֵ   יִ   לִ   שִׁ
(5)   (4)   (3)   (2)   (1)

＿＿＿

LAHMED ל

Yes, the **LAHMED** is different.

It begins *above* the line:

step 3   step 2   step 1

You try:

---

top

Place a ✓ next to the correct answer:

☐ The vowel O וֹ as in **TORAH** is written below the line.

☐ The vowel O וֹ as in **TORAH** is written on the line.

Y

YUD י is smaller than any other Hebrew letter and does not reach down to the bottom line.

The saying sound of **YUD** is _____.

אֶל
or
אֵל

AHL

The names of our two **SILENT LETTERS** are **AHLEF** and **AHYIN**. How many times does the **AHYIN** appear below?

ע א ע א ע ע א ע א ע ע

_____ times

Helpful hints:

וֹ = O וּ = OO : = SILENT

Here's a tricky one:

Read each syllable aloud, then copy the letter and vowel with the sound G:

גוּ גְ גַ גוּ גָ גוֹ ←

Write your answer here: _____

GAH גַ

Remember, the name of every letter begins with its saying sound.

The name of this letter ח is CHET.

This letter ח, with the saying sound of CH, is called _____ .

CH

CHAHF is written כ.

KAHF is written _____ .

KAHF כּ

לִי is a real Hebrew word, meaning "to me."

We use the LAHMED, the vowel IH, and the YUD to create לִי , which we read _____ .

שׁיּ SEE

ל ל ל

Let's practice a little more. This time we'll include the MEM מ.

In each space below, write the correct letter:

LAHMED   MEM   MEM   LAHMED

__ __   ___   ___   __ __
___   ___

---

on the line
(#2)

The vowel וֹ, with the dot on top, is _____ as in _____.

Y

י has the saying sound of Y and is called _____.

7

This is how to write the **SILENT LETTER AHYIN:** ע

ע   ل   ı
step 3   step 2   step 1

Now it's your turn:

____ ____ ____ ____ ע

G
AH

The sound of this letter and vowel גֶ is _____ .

CH

Are you finding it difficult to pronounce the CH ח as in CHANUKAH? Some people do. Maybe you know the sound from the name of the special Sabbath bread, CHAHLAH (commonly spelled CHALLAH). Both CHANUKAH and CHAHLAH begin with the letter ח. Its saying sound is _____ .

KAHF כֿ

Whenever we add a dot in Hebrew, the saying sound gets shorter and harder. The saying sound of כ is CH.
But the saying sound of כּ is K. כֿ is called _____ .

REE רִי

This שִ reads SIH.
Here is SEE: ____

ל LAHMED

מ MEM

מ MEM

ל LAHMED

Read the following line aloud. How many times does the sound **LAH** appear?

לַ לֶ לָ לֶ לַ לֶ ←

_____ times

O as in

TORAH

וֹ

Sometimes the vowel וֹ (*O* as in TORAH) appears only as a dot, like this: ˙

We will always write it the full way, like this: וֹ.

Let's practice writing the new vowel *O* וֹ as in TORAH:

וֹ   ו   ˙

step 3   step 2   step 1

וֹ

_____   _____   _____

YUD

י

The letter **YUD** is written this way:

—י—   —˙—

_____   _____

step 2   step 1

_____ _____ _____ —י—

Let's practice: _____ _____ _____ _____

ע ע ע

AHYIN is written _____ .

AHLEF is written _____ .

ג ג ג

GIMMEL ג has the saying sound of _____ , and ָ has the sound _____ as in OOMPAH.

CHANUKAH

The saying sound of this Hebrew letter ח, which does not appear in the English alphabet, is _____ .

CHAHF כּ

This letter with the dot כּ is called _____ .

Hint: Its saying sound is K.

מִ MIH

When we combine ר and . , we have the sound RIH.

This syllable רִ reads _____ .

4

Remember, both
 ָ and ֵ are
AH as in *OOMPAH*.

Read each sound aloud, then put a ☐ around the sound **LAY**:

מָ לַ מֶ לֵ ⟵

וֹ וֹ וֹ

שׁ and וֹ combine to make שׁוֹ , which has the sound **SHO**.

This letter and vowel combination לוֹ has the sound _____ .

י י י

Put a ✓ in the correct circle:

◯ **YUD** *does not* reach the bottom line.

◯ **YUD** *does* reach the bottom line.

◯ **YUD** reaches *below* the bottom line.

עַ   AHYIN

אַ   AHLEF

Since we read both עַ and אַ as AH, we read both עוֹ and אוֹ as _____ .

GIMMEL
G as in GO

ג

The **GIMMEL** has the saying sound of **G** and is written ג.

ג step 2   ו step 1

Now you try:

___ ___ ___ _ג_

CH

This letter ח has the saying sound of **CH** as in

_____ .

KAHF

כּ

KAHF כּ has a dot in the middle.

If we leave out the dot כ, the letter is _____ .

EE

ִי

Here is the syllable **MEE**: מִי

Here is the syllable **MIH**: _____

לַ

LAY

Using this vowel **AH** ָ , write the letter and vowel with the sound **LAH**:

_____

LO   לוֹ

When we add **FINAL MEM** ם to the letter and vowel לוֹ, we read לוֹם.

Write its sound here: _____

YUD
does not reach
the bottom line.

You know that י has the saying sound of **Y**, and that ָ is the vowel **AH** as in **OOMPAH**.

The letter and vowel combination יָ has the sound _____.

O

Read these sounds aloud:

AH   AH   AY   OI   OOI
ָ   ַ   ֵ

Now circle the syllables that read **AY**:

אֶ   אוֹ   אוֹ   אֲ   אַ   אֲ   אַ

GIMMEL ג

ג is called _____ and has the saying sound of _____ as in _____ .

עֶ֫רֶב

EH-REHV

Hebrew has one sound that English does not. Still, you've heard and said it many times.

The letter ח has the saying sound of **CH** as in **CHANUKAH**.

The Hebrew sound that English doesn't have is _____ .

6

Remember how **VET** כ became **BET** בּ when we added a dot?

Here we go again with **CHAHF** כ. Add a dot כּ, and the letter is called **KAHF**.

כּ is called _____ .

KEE כִּי

We now know that ִ has the sound **IH**, except when it appears like so: ִי, when its sound is _____ .

לְ   LAH

Using this vowel AH ַ, write these two syllables:

LAH   MAH

____   ____

(2)   (1)

LOM   לוֹם

We just added the ם *after* the לוֹ to read LOM לוֹם.

Suppose we write שָׁ *before* the LOM, like this: שָׁלוֹם.

What well-known word can you read now? _____

YAH   יָ

Read the following line. Which syllable has the sound YOO?

יִ   יֻן   יוֹן   יָ   יַ ←

5   4   3   2   1

Write the number here: ____

AY

You remember that this ב is the VET and this ם is the FINAL MEM.

Here are two words. We'll write the sound under the first one. You write the sound under the other.

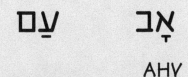

עַם   אָב

____   AHV

G

The letter with the saying sound of **G** as in **GO** is written
λ and is called **G** __ __ __ __ **L**.

#2 רֶ

When we write the syllables עֶ and רֶ and add **VET** ב,
we get the Hebrew word for "evening":

עֶרֶב

Write its sound here: _____

ך CHAHF

Put a ✓ over each **CHAHF** below:

ך   ב   ב   ך   ב   ב   ך   ב   ב   ך

How many did you ✓? _____

YIH

Here is the letter **YUD** י.

Sometimes the **YUD** י stands by itself *after* a letter and
the vowel **IH** ִ : מִי כִּי

In these cases, **IH** becomes **EE**.

So if we read the word מִי as **MEE**, we read the word
כִּי as _____.

Read each line aloud.

Which one reads MAH LAH MAY?

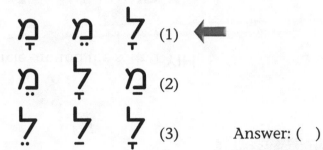

(1) ←

(2)

(3)   Answer: ( )

(2) (1)

LAH MAH

Good for you! Ready to combine two words?

Remember the Hebrew word for Sabbath, שַׁבָּת ?

Sometimes it is written שַׁבַּת .

Let's add שָׁלוֹם to it, to make a Sabbath greeting:

שַׁבָּת שָׁלוֹם ←

It reads SHA_____ _____OM.

SHAH-LOM
(commonly spelled
SHALOM)

שָׁלוֹם

Draw a line to connect each matching set:

YAY   יְ

YO   יוֹ

YAH   יָ

#4   יוֹ

The Hebrew word AH-MAYN (commonly spelled AMEN) is also an English word.

Fill in the correct vowels to make this word read AMEN:

אמן

עַם

AHM

Lesson 9: Frame 9

X
ג

G as in *GO*

ג is called **GIMMEL** and has the saying sound of ____ as in *GO*.

Lesson 10: Frame 9

EH — עֶ

One of these sounds reads **REH**. Which one?

Read them aloud:

4	3	2	1
עֶ	אֶ	רֶ	גֶ

______

Lesson 11: Frame 9

כַ CHAH

Sometimes the **VET** ב is confused with the **CHAHF** כ.
Be careful!

VET is written ב.

CHAHF is written ____.

Lesson 12: Frame 9

אִ עִ

IH IH

Draw a circle around the sound **YIH**:

אִ מִ גִ יִ

(2)

You know how to read all the Hebrew syllables below.

Read them aloud, then copy the one with the sound **SHAY**:

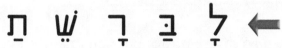

תַ שֶׁ רְ בַ לָ ←

_____

**SHABBAT
SHALOM**

שַׁבָּת
שָׁלוֹם

וֹ has the sound **O** as in **TORAH**. Here is the second vowel that is not written below the line: וּ. It has a dot in the middle and has the sound **OO** as in **FOOD**.

The vowel **OO** וּ as in **FOOD** has a dot in the

_____.

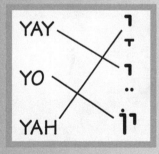

YAY — יֹ

YO — יֵ

YAH — יַ

When we combine י and ַ , we create יַ , which has the sound **YAH**.

Now read this: יוֹ

Write its sound here: _____

AMEN

אָמֵן
or
אָמֵן

You know that the Hebrew alphabet has two **SILENT LETTERS**, **AHLEF** א and **AHYIN** ע.

The Hebrew alphabet also has one **SILENT VOWEL**.

This ___ is the **SILENT VOWEL**.

Circle the **SILENT VOWEL**:   א   ְ   ע

ְנ   ְנ   ְנ

#1 and #5 and #6

These two Hebrew letters look very much alike:

נ has the saying sound of N.

ג has the saying sound of G as in GO.

Put an X over the letter with the saying sound of G as in GO:

ג   נ

גֶּ   GEH

You remember that AHLEF א and AHYIN ע are SILENT LETTERS.

When we add our new vowel ֶ to the AHYIN ע, like this: עֶ, we read _____ .

CHO   כוֹ

Helpful hint: ֶ = EH   ַ = AH

This is CHEH: כֶ

This is CHAH: _____ (use CHAHF)

גִ   GIH

Here's a tricky one: The AHLEF א and the AHYIN ע have no sound. Under each letter and vowel below, write the sound of the syllable:

אֶ   עִ

_____   _____
(2)   (1)

שַׁ SHAY

Draw a circle around the syllable that has the sound SAH:

מָ שַׁ דֵ בְ תַ

middle

Copy the vowel that has the sound OO as in FOOD:

וֹ וֹ

_____

YO יוֹ

Ready for the next step?

Add the FINAL MEM ם to יוֹ, and you get

יוֹם,

as in the High Holy Day, _____ Kippur.

: is the SILENT _____.

It is called SH'VAH.

NOO נוּ

The sound **NAH** appears three times below.

Which numbers are they?

נוּ   בַ   נַ   נֶ   נוּ   נְ   נַ
7   6   5   4   3   2   1

#_____ and #_____ and #_____

NEH נֶ

Write the letter and vowel with the sound **GEH**: _____

כ CHAHF

When we combine the CHAHF כ and the vowel OO וּ,
we create CHOO כוּ.

How do we read this syllable: כוּ?

_____

DIH דִ

GEH is written גֶ.

GIH is written _____.

SAH

If your answer was incorrect, go back and reread the last frame.

Ready to learn a new Hebrew word?

LAYV is the Hebrew word for heart.

This is how we write it: לֵב

    Its first letter is called _____ .

    Its vowel is _____ as in _____ .

    Its last letter is called _____ .

וֹ   OO

The vowel that is written on the line and has a dot in the middle has the sound _____ as in _____ .

YOM   יוֹם

Here is a new **FINAL LETTER: FINAL NUN.** ‗ן‗

FINAL NUN goes below the line ‗ן‗ , not like VAHV ‗ו‗ or YUD ‗י‗ .

This letter ‗ן‗ is FINAL _____ .

VOWEL

The **SILENT VOWEL,** written like this: ְ , has no sound and is called **SH'**_____ .

Vowels we know:

AH   AH   AY   SILENT   O   OO

The sound of נֵ is NAY.

The sound of נוּ is _____ .

3

You know that **NUN** is written נ and that

GIMMEL is written ג.

When we write גְ, the sound is _____ .

CHET is written ח.

CHAHF is written _____ .

4

Here is **DAHLET** ד. When we combine it with the vowel **AY** ֵ, like this: דֵ, it reads **DAY**.

This sound דּ reads _____ .

LAHMED	ל
AY as in DAY	ֵ
VET	ב

The Hebrew word for heart, לֵב , is written LAHMED, AY as in DAY, and VET.

So לֵב has the combined sound

_____ .

OO as in FOOD	וּ

How many times does the vowel with the sound OO as in FOOD appear below?

וֹ וּ וֹ וּ וֹ וּ וֹ וֹ וּ

_____ times

FINAL NUN	ן

FINAL NUN appears only at the end of a word and has the saying sound of N.

Write a FINAL NUN here: _____

SH'VAH	ְ

Here are the vowels you know. Put a ✓ over each SH'VAH:

ְ ַ ָ ֵ ַ ְ ֵ ָ ְ

How many ✓'s? _____

end

This is how we write the **NUN**:

] step 2   1 step 1

Practice a few: _____ _____ _____]

EH

How many times does the vowel **EH** appear below?

_____ times

CHAHF]

Let's practice writing **CHAHF**]:

___ ___ ___]

IH

How many times does the vowel **IH** . as in **TICK** appear below?

_____ times

LAYV לֵב

Now you write the Hebrew word for heart:

_____

5

Let's build another word.

You remember that the syllable לוֹ has the sound LO.

The syllable לוֹ has the sound _____ .

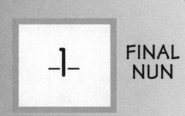
FINAL NUN

Did you remember to bring it below the line?

The letter VAHV is written *on* the line. ⁄נ⁄

FINAL NUN goes *below* the line. ⁄ן⁄

How many FINAL NUNs in this row?

⁄נ⁄ ⁄ן⁄ ⁄נ⁄ ⁄ן⁄ ⁄ן⁄

Answer here: _____

3

We call this SILENT VOWEL ְ SH'VAH. It has no sound and is written *under* the letter.

Place a SH'VAH under the SHIN שׁ .

NUN]

The NUN] is used at the beginning or middle of a word.

The FINAL NUN] appears only at the _____ of a word.

EH as in PET

The vowel EH always appears under a letter and is written _____.

CH

This letter Π is called CHET.

This letter] is called _____.

TICK

Like all vowels except O] and OO], the vowel IH as in TICK is written under the line.

Write it here: _____

לֵב   LAYV

Do you remember that we read שַׁבָּת as SHABBAT?

How about the first word you learned?
We read בַּד as _____.

LOO   לוֹ

When we combine the vowel AH ָ with the letter ל, like this: לָ , we read _____.

3

Let's review all the new letters:

YUD י does not reach the bottom line.

VAHV ו reaches the bottom line.

FINAL NUN ן goes _____ the bottom line.

שׁ   SH

In this group of syllables, which one reads MAH? Read them aloud:

מַ תָ בֵ לְ שֶׁ ←

Write it here: _____

N

כ has the saying sound of N and is called _____ .

PET

What is the sound of ּ ? _____ as in _____

CHET ח

Both CHAHF כ and CHET ח have the saying sound of _____ .

IH .

. has the sound IH as in _____ .

BAR   בַּר

Let's review some words you learned. One of the words below reads **LAYV**. Read each word aloud, then place a ✓ over the word **LAYV**:

לֵב   שַׁבָּת   בַּר   ←

LAH   לְ

Now we'll add the **VET** ב to לְ and לוֹ to form לוֹלְב, which reads _____.

below

Draw a circle around each **FINAL NUN** in the row below:

ן   י   ן   ן   ן   ן   ן   י   ן

How many circles in the row? _____

מַ   MAH

Here is a word that may look familiar.
(Remember what you learned about **AHYIN**.)

Do you recognize this word? שְׁמַע

The word is _____.

Check your answer here:

]

NUN

The saying sound of NUN] is _____.

Check your answer here:

3

.. has the saying sound EH as in _____.

Check your answer here:

CH

ⴺ is called CHAHF, and ⨅ is called _____.

Check your answer here:

1

What is the sound of the vowel . ?

_____